TRUE TEEN STORIES

TRUE STORIES OF
Teen Homelessness

Monika Davies

Cavendish Square

New York

Published in 2018 by Cavendish Square Publishing, LLC
243 5th Avenue, Suite 136, New York, NY 10016

Website: cavendishsq.com

This publication represents the opinions and views of the author based on his or her personal experience, knowledge, and research. The information in this book serves as a general guide only. The author and publisher have used their best efforts in preparing this book and disclaim liability rising directly or indirectly from the use and application of this book.

All websites were available and accurate when this book was sent to press.

Cataloging-in-Publication Data

Names: Davies, Monika.
Title: True stories of teen homelessness / Monika Davies.
Description: New York : Cavendish Square, 2018. | Series: True teen stories | Includes bibliographical references and index.
Identifiers: ISBN 9781502634023 (pbk.) | ISBN 9781502631589 (library bound) | ISBN 9781502631596 (ebook)
Subjects: LCSH: Homeless teenagers--Juvenile literature. | Homelessness--Juvenile literature.
Classification: LCC HV4493 .D38 2018 | DDC 362.7'75692083--dc23

Editorial Director: David McNamara
Editor: Caitlyn Miller
Copy Editor: Alex Tessman
Associate Art Director: Amy Greenan
Designer: Seth Hughes
Production Coordinator: Karol Szymczuk
Photo Research: J8 Media

The photographs in this book are used by permission and through the courtesy of: Cover Matt Mawson/Corbis/Getty Images; p. 4 Nick Beer/Shutterstock.com; p. 8 In Pictures Ltd./Corbis/Getty Images; p. 10 Zuma Press/Alamy Stock Photo; p. 13 ImageGallery2/Alamy Stock Photo; p. 15 Jonas Gratzer/LightRocket/Getty Images; p. 18 Ira Berger/Alamy Stock Photo; p. 24 R.Nagy/Shutterstock.com; p. 26 Noel Celis/AFP/Getty Images; p. 30 Reuters/Alamy Stock Photo; p. 31 Peter Charlesworth/LightRocket/Getty Images; p. 34 Mrmohock/Shutterstock.com; p. 36 Christine Osborne Pictures/Alamy Stock Photo; p. 37 Paula Bronstein/Getty Images; p. 41 Walterericsy/Shutterstock.com; p. 46 Romrodphoto/Shutterstock.com; p. 49 Lane V. Erickson/Shutterstock.com; p. 51 DBImages/Alamy Stock Photo; p. 52 Michael Schwartz/New York Post Archives/NYP Holdings, Inc./Getty Images; p. 54 Custom Life Science Images/Alamy Stock Photo; p. 58 Ocean Morisset; p. 63 T photography/Shutterstock.com; p. 64 William Sutton/Danita Delimont/Alamy Stock Photo; p. 67 Agencia Fotograficzna Caro/Alamy Stock Photo; p. 70 John Wollwert/Shutterstock.com; p. 75 Bernat Armangue/AP Images; p. 78 David Klepper/AP Images; p. 81 Christos Georghiou/Shutterstock.com; p. 85 Minnesota Public Radio, Rupa Shenoy/AP Images; p. 91 Pazut Wutigornsombatkul/Shutterstock.com; p. 93 Jason Gutierrez/AFP/Getty Images; p. 95 Joe Scarnici/Getty Images for generationOn.

Manufactured in China

CONTENTS

Invisible and Isolated

I n 2014, the Make Them Visible Foundation conducted and filmed a social experiment. The resulting study intended to answer the following question: "Have the homeless become so invisible [that] we wouldn't notice our own family members living on the street?"

Set up in New York City, the foundation asked relatives of various longtime New York residents to dress up as homeless individuals for the day. The relatives—sisters, mothers, and uncles of the residents—then sat on street corners that the residents passed every day. One by one, each of the New Yorkers walked past their family members: people they knew, respected, and loved—and didn't notice them. Most of them hardly glanced at the people they thought were part of New York's homeless population.

Homelessness is an issue all around the world. But, for such a **pervasive** and global issue, homelessness is a topic often

Opposite: Worldwide, millions of homeless teenagers face an uncertain future when they live on the streets without safe, permanent shelter.

misunderstood and unacknowledged. Individuals and families who are homeless find themselves ignored in their own communities. They are invisible; and often, they are utterly isolated.

In the most basic sense, being homeless means that one doesn't have a home. A more in-depth definition refers to an individual or family's lack of a constant, safe, and warm shelter. But being homeless translates to more than a simple lack of shelter. For homeless people around the world, it also denotes a lack of stability, the increased risk of health problems, and exposure to a litany of other concerns. Homeless individuals are some of the most vulnerable of a country's population, and perhaps the most vulnerable set of any homeless population is its teenagers.

THREE CITIES, MULTIPLE STORIES

"You worry about freezing to death. You worry about being robbed and beaten up … about where you're going to get something to eat."
—Karen, fifteen years old (Covenant House, Toronto, 2012)

Entering your teenage years signals the beginning of substantial change and growth. It means growing up physically, emotionally, and mentally, and this puts a heady number of stressors on young adults. It's a lot to handle for any young adult. Some teenagers dealing with these multiple new stressors are also growing up homeless. It can be difficult to understand not only how this vulnerable population copes but also how they became homeless in the first place.

When it comes to understanding any issue, it's logical to start at the beginning with history and numbers. That's where we'll start, but statistics only give a clinical—though startling—view of the issue of homelessness. To dive deeper, we'll spend time meeting young adults living on the streets in three cities around the world and learning more about their lives.

First, we'll examine cases of homeless teens in Manila, the capital of the Philippines, which is one of the most densely populated cities in the world. This population density—and the poor living conditions of the city's slums—leads to many teenagers sleeping in cemeteries and eating garbage from dump sites to stay alive.

Next, we'll move New York City, which happens to have one of the highest homeless populations across the United States. Here, we'll look at the city's growing homeless population, while meeting homeless teenagers who identify as part of the **LGBTQIA+** community. Homeless LGBTQIA+ teenagers are some of the most at-risk homeless youth, and the hardships they face are specific and unique to them.

Finally, we will explore Nairboi, Kenya, a city with thousands of young teenagers living on the streets, most of whom are coping with dangerous addictions. These homeless youths are struggling to find a way to combat the hunger and misery of being alone on the streets, but, unfortunately, this often translates into risky addictions. These teenagers face a community that is less than understanding, which makes it difficult for them to get help when they need it most.

Being homeless while tackling the growing pains of your teenage years makes for a complicated and isolated upbringing. Youth homelessness is an issue with multiple facets and deserves global attention. The stories of homeless teenagers are all their own, and all deserve to be told and heard.

CHAPTER ONE

Teen Homelessness Today

Today's homeless teenagers live across the globe, each with a story to tell. The perspectives of young adults living on the streets are just starting to surface. For too long, homeless "unaccompanied" youth were uncounted, unnoticed, and among the most vulnerable of the homeless population. Now, the number of homeless teenagers is starting to get counted and noted in research studies. And the numbers are startling.

NUMBER CRUNCHING: AMERICAN STATISTICS

Tallying up the numbers of teenagers living on the streets, in America and worldwide, is a near impossible task, and accumulated statistics are almost guaranteed to be inaccurate.

Opposite: At the Wema Centre in Kenya, homeless youth line up to receive a simple meal of rice and beans.

Most reports count the number of teenagers relying on shelter beds, while also adding up the number of youth sleeping on park benches or a sidewalk curb. However, this doesn't account for teenagers who are drifting from couch to couch, or a young adult who is perhaps too ashamed to admit they are homeless. Out of necessity, homeless youth and families are often mobile, and this makes it difficult to gather an accurate count of the number of homeless teenagers in any given community.

Reports vary wildly, but Youth.gov estimates that every year there are between five hundred thousand to 2.8 million teenagers who are homeless in the United States. In comparison, the Covenant House places their estimate at two million teenagers in the United States who experience at least a period of homelessness every year.

In Modesto, California, volunteers chat with a homeless teenager as part of 2016's Point-in-Time Count.

Every other year, the United States Department of Housing and Urban Development (HUD) asks cities across America to tally the number of homeless individuals in their respective communities on one single night in January. These are known as **Point-in-Time Counts**. These counts are a form of data collection that gives insight into the number of people who are homeless across the United States. Recently, this data collection has begun to count the number of "unaccompanied" youth who are living on the streets. These are homeless young adults under the age of twenty-five who do not have a parent or guardian with them.

In January 2016, the Point-in-Time count tallied 549,928 people who were experiencing homelessness across the United States. Around 68 percent had some form of shelter—meaning they were housed in a safe haven, an emergency shelter, or in a transitional housing program—while 32 percent were unsheltered and living on the streets.

Of the over half a million people homeless on that January night, 35,686 of them were unaccompanied homeless youth, or 7 percent of the total homeless population. The majority—89 percent of the unaccompanied homeless youth tallied—were eighteen to twenty-four years old. Of course, these statistics are likely far below the true totals, especially when it comes to counting the number of homeless teenagers living on the streets. Studies have shown that teenagers are more likely to hide their homelessness, especially as many want to fit in with their peers and keep their personal struggles hidden.

Data from the United States Department of Education offers an interesting comparison point. During the 2013–2014 school year, the department released their data regarding the total number of homeless students enrolled in local education agencies. At the time, the national total was 1,360,747 students who were experiencing homelessness.

Clearly, the statistics are murky and undefined. Yet it's important for these statistics to continue to be counted, as this helps effect real change in policies and understanding. It's promising that an effort is being made to count the homeless youth population, especially in America. In the United States, a clearer understanding of youth homelessness is developing. However, while this is a positive change, it is only the first step in combating the problem.

NUMBER CRUNCHING: WORLDWIDE STATISTICS

"I left school after my father died and my mother couldn't afford to take me to school[.] I thought it was easier to go out and take care of myself. I want to go back to school one day ... I don't want to be here [on the streets] for the rest of my life."
—Neville, thirteen years old (BBC, Nairobi, 2015)

Worldwide, the number of homeless youth living on the streets is several magnitudes higher. Based on various sources, the United Nations believes there are up to 150 million **street children** around the world. This is a hotly contested fact, though, and other estimates place that number around 100 million, instead—which is still an unfortunately high statistic. The term "street children" refers to youth who spend most of their time living and working on their city's streets.

In the Philippines, thousands of children live on the streets, completely vulnerable to the elements.

These are young children and teenagers who work the streets: begging, scavenging, and providing services for a source of income. Some have a family to return to at the end of the day, while others are alone. These homeless youth are especially **susceptible** to abuse, exploitation, and violence. They often have the shortest life expectancies and face a bleak future.

UNDERSTANDING HOMELESSNESS

These statistics are upsetting and, hopefully, eye-opening. Although examining the youth homelessness statistics begins to give us an idea as to the depth of the issue, it often leads to the logical next question: why are these teenagers homeless? The simplified answer is that constant, safe shelter is not an affordable option for those who experience homelessness. However, diving into the reasons and nuances behind the "why" of unaffordable housing makes for a much more complicated answer.

Every homeless individual, including young teenagers, has their own story as to why they lack a permanent shelter. A homeless teenager in the Philippines faces a completely unique set of difficulties when compared to a homeless teenager in America. Invariably, a homeless teenager's community and culture colors and defines the reasons they are without a place to call home. Depending on where a teenager lives, the resources and opportunities available to them will differ, as will general societal **perceptions**.

We need to be careful when making sweeping generalizations about the reasons behind homelessness. This can easily lead to ill-conceived perceptions about the state of the issue worldwide. It's important to always remember that every situation and story is a patchwork quilt of details—no two are alike. Yet there are some common reasons as to why someone might end up homeless. Identifying these broad concerns can help us figure out ways to help.

FACING HOMELESSNESS TOGETHER: TEENAGERS WITH HOMELESS FAMILIES

A teenager who is homeless with their family is sharing their experience alongside their parents and siblings. If a teenager's family is homeless, root causes often tie back to issues that concern their family's history or living conditions.

When parents or guardians struggle to make ends meet, their entire family can wind up living on the streets.

For teenagers growing up in families based in developing countries like the Philippines, the cause of their homelessness is often a struggle with **poverty**. Many families do not have the funds to feed and shelter their family. They end up living on the streets to make ends meet. Growing up in poverty is not an issue unique to developing countries, though. In the United States (and other "developed" nations), there are many families who are too poor to afford proper housing and enough food to feed their entire family. Often, a lack of affordable housing in the community for families with a lower income is to blame. According to the United States Department of Housing and Urban Development, if more than 30 percent of a family's income is put toward housing costs, they are considered **cost-burdened**. This means they are paying too much for housing and will find it difficult to pay for food, clothing, transportation, and other necessities for their families.

HUD estimates that in the United States there are over twelve million households that spend more than 50 percent of their family's income on housing. Considering the cost of food, clothing, and transportation, this then leaves alarmingly little money for them to meet their other needs. HUD also states that if a family has only one parent or guardian who is working full time at the federal minimum wage (which, as of 2017, is $7.25 per hour), they won't be able to afford a two-bedroom apartment in *any* city in the United States.

The stress of growing up in a family who cannot afford a stable, consistent shelter is immeasurable. If a young teenager's family is struggling financially, the teen will likely begin looking for work as soon as they are able to do so. Working part time while attending school can make for a complicated and stressful schedule for any young adult.

It is also common for teenagers growing up homeless to live **transient** lives. Many homeless families are forced to move from place to place or from shelter to shelter in the hope of better work opportunities. For instance, a family may move from their rural home to the city, hoping that the urban environment will be more favorable for their living situation. Furthermore, in the United States, there are relatively few family shelters, which means a family is often split up to accommodate all individual family members.

A transient lifestyle lacks stability, which is what most people—especially maturing young adults—need most. Being constantly on the move and having to deal with new environments on a regular basis adds stress and uncertainty, emotions that can complicate the already tumultuous teenage experience.

ON THEIR OWN

While some teenagers wind up homeless alongside their families, homeless teenagers are frequently living on the streets with no one's support but their own. The decision to live on the streets is not an easy one for most teenagers. More often, it is not a decision teenagers have made for themselves at all.

While the Point-in-Time Count officially tallied 35,686 unaccompanied youth on a single night in January 2016, the actual number is guaranteed to be much higher. Many homeless teenagers live in fear of falling into the **child welfare system**, so they hide their homeless living situation from prying eyes.

As previously mentioned, the United States Department of Education counted over a million students who were experiencing homelessness in the 2013–2014 school year. But the study also kept track of the number of unaccompanied homeless youth who were enrolled in school: 88,966 students in total. Of course, this number does not account for homeless youth who were not participating or enrolled in the education system, but it does indicate that the number of unaccompanied, homeless youth is likely much higher than "Point-in-Time" statistics show.

Living on the streets is often a very lonely, isolating experience for homeless teenagers.

Most of the time, teenagers who end up homeless on their own are running away from the people who should be their greatest support system: their family. The majority of unaccompanied homeless teenagers cite family issues as the reason they are living on the streets or floating from couch to couch. These family issues range from domestic violence to parental substance abuse to a rejection of a youth's **sexual orientation** and **gender identity**.

Studies have shown that between 21 to 43 percent of teenagers who run away from home are fleeing an abusive household. Often, it is young female teenagers who run away from home, suffering from sexual and/or physical abuse. Several studies have also shown that up to 40 percent of homeless teenagers identify as part of the LGBTQIA+ community. This is a critical statistic to take note of. Research has shown that LGBTQIA+ youth are often homeless due to a lack of acceptance from family members. And this lack of acceptance frequently manifests into physical or emotional abuse from the teenager's guardians, leading LGBTQIA+ teenagers to choose a life on the streets.

Another common reason why a teenager ends up homeless is because they were previously in the child welfare system. It is estimated that between 12 to 36 percent of all homeless youth are on the streets because they have "aged out" of the system, which means they have had to exit the foster care system because they turned eighteen. Many end up moving from place to place, as they are suddenly expected to have the skill set to make it on their own. Yet many do not have the funds or ability to support themselves individually. Instead, they end up homeless and alone, without any kind of support system to turn to.

EFFECTS AND CONSEQUENCES

More and more, governments and policy makers are examining the statistics surrounding youth homelessness and acknowledging the gravity of the situation. This is crucial for finding solutions to teen homelessness. While we can guess at the physical, emotional, and mental costs of being homeless—especially during your formative teenage years—the actual numbers present an even more dire portrait.

According to the National Conference of State Legislatures (NCLS), a bipartisan non-governmental organization, homeless teenagers are at a higher risk for "physical abuse, sexual exploitation, mental health disabilities, substance abuse, and death." They estimate that five thousand homeless American teenagers die "as a result of assault, illness, or suicide" every year.

Being homeless has a direct impact on your physical and mental health, both in the short-term and the long-term. Short-term, there are the obvious dangers of living on the streets. A young, homeless teenager is unprotected from the elements, while also easily preyed upon by older peers. However, the consequences of experiencing homelessness also reach past the time spent on the streets. For many adults who experienced homelessness as a teenager, there is a long list of long-term health and mental consequences.

Many teenagers who are homeless suffer from high anxiety, depression, and cripplingly low self-esteem. These are debilitating feelings that often worsen as they mature. The National Runaway Safeline (NRS), a national communications system that helps young runaways, points out a study that found people who were teenage runaways were 51 percent more likely to consider suicide as an adult. Teenage runaways were also three times more likely to attempt suicide in adulthood and three times more likely to deal with mental health problems. Yet according to the National Network for Youth, only about 9 percent of teenage runaways will gain access to mental health services.

Dealing with the multitude of stressors that arise from being homeless also leads many young teenagers on the streets to begin using drugs. This adversely affects their overall health, and substance abuse only increases as the stress of their situation grows. A former teenage runaway is 2.4 times more likely to pick up a smoking habit, 67 percent more likely to use marijuana, and 18 times more likely to use crack cocaine. Between 30 to 40 percent of homeless teenagers deal with an alcohol addiction later in life.

Homeless teenagers are also much more likely to resort to criminal activity to stay alive. Studies have shown that 23 percent of homeless teenagers have stolen items, while 20 percent have dealt drugs. Resorting to criminal activity is often a self-preservation tactic for homeless teenagers, who find themselves in a financially desperate situation. They are cornered with no way out. Engaging in criminal activity is risky, extremely dangerous, and illegal, and sadly, many homeless teenagers find themselves on the wrong side of the law. They end up contending with the criminal justice system at a very young age, which hurts their chances of rebuilding their lives in a meaningful way.

When a teenager is homeless, most of the time they can only focus on a day at a time and placing one foot in front of the other. Their sole focus is on survival. Finding a place to sleep and food to eat are their primary concerns. To meet these survival needs, many will go to extreme measures, especially when they lack a support system that would give them alternatives.

Perhaps the most tragic consequence of experiencing homelessness for teenagers is their loss of future opportunities. Many homeless youth are unable to finish high school, and most don't have the funds to attend a post-secondary school. They lack the stable lifestyle needed to keep a financially secure job, which means they are also unlikely to acquire the work experience needed for a higher paying job. These multiple factors severely limit a teenager's adult career potential, setting them up to suffer financially in the future. A 2011 study found that adults who had been teenage runaways made, on average, $8,823 less per year than adults who had never experienced homelessness.

The ramifications of being homeless are numerous and devastating. Support and understanding for homeless teenagers is growing and developing, especially in America, but a lot of change—and further education—is needed before youth homelessness can be properly addressed. However, one simple way we can build understanding is to the listen to the stories of homeless teenagers. In the following case studies, you'll find the stories of homeless teenagers living in Manila, New York City, and Nairobi, gaining a small window into their lives and what their specific needs are.

TEEN HOMELESSNESS IN THE NEWS

Often, news media highlights the "success stories" of teenagers who were previously homeless but worked their way to becoming their class valedictorian or have since received a substantial scholarship to attend college. While these stories are heart-warming, there also needs to be a focus on the stories of homeless teenagers who haven't been as successful at beating the odds. Sharing the stories of youth who are still struggling with life on the streets allows for more expansive detail to the issue of teen homelessness. Stories of struggle also encourage readers to focus on how they can help.

One way change occurs is when a conversation around an issue expands and grows. Greater news coverage of the state of homelessness in North America and worldwide would help significantly in affecting policies and understanding around the causes and solutions to this issue. Furthermore, articles on teen homelessness, which feature the voices and stories of youth living without shelter, have the potential to jumpstart the conversation on different ways we can positively help young people.

CHAPTER TWO

Homeless Teens in Manila

If you sneak a peek at Manila's skyline, you might think that the city is built out of skyscrapers. These sleek towers bump up against the sky, gleaming bright in the sunlight. Suited-up working professionals duck in and out of buildings that run dozens of stories high. This dashing skyline trumpets a modernized Manila, the capital city of a country with a soaring global future in its sights. But Manila is not a city built out of skyscrapers. Rather, it is a city of people. It is a city overflowing—and filled to the brim—with people.

Once your eyes climb back down from these towering skyscrapers and you begin moving out of Manila's downtown core, the city's story shifts. Step away from this downtown district, and you begin to walk down streets layered with makeshift tin houses, some balanced precariously on stilts in water. Lines of tattered clothing crisscross thin, tight alleyways.

Opposite: Manila, the Philippines' capital city, is filled with economic promise. However, many of its citizens face a less promising future.

Manila's slums are a stark, startling contrast to the gleaming skyscrapers of the city's downtown core.

The neighborhoods are bordered with enormous dump sites, each littered with a dark mish-mash of mud and waste. Soon, among the beeping of horns and squawking of chickens, you'll hear the hum and chatter of thousands of voices. There are people everywhere: young, old, and everyone in between, and they are all crowded into this cramped, chaotic world. Welcome to the slums of Manila. This is where the stories of many of Manila's homeless teenagers begin.

ZEROING IN ON A CROWDED POPULATION

To understand the stories of Manila's homeless teens, it's important to look at where many begin their lives, which is in the city's slums. Here it is easy to see firsthand one of the hard truths the country is facing: there are so many children—and there still isn't enough support for them.

The Philippines has become known on the world stage for its elbow-to-elbow population density. Population density refers to the number of people in a specific location. In Manila's most populous slums, the density of population towers at a world record high, with over fifty-one thousand people per square kilometer. For perspective, consider the crowds that pave the streets of New York City. The Big Apple has the highest population density for an American city, yet it records an "uncrowded" density of about twenty-seven thousand people per square mile.

A rising population density is a primary concern for Manila, as the city has seen staggering development growth over the last fifteen years. In 2015, the city's population density registered a 30 percent rise from 2000's statistics. And the city's crowds will only continue to grow tighter and tighter.

Manila, now considered a "megacity" with more than ten million citizens, ranks as one of the most crowded cities in the world. This climbing population poses a new set of questions for the city and its country, namely: are they prepared to support this huge increase in their population with the proper **infrastructure** and support? The answers are mixed.

ASIA'S STRONGEST ECONOMIC GROWTH

The Philippines is dealing with a rocketing economic growth. According to *Bloomberg*, the Philippines is the "fastest-expanding" economy in the world. The country's global nickname is the "rising tiger."

The Philippines has pushed for the globalization of its economy, which means many Filipino businesses are now operating on an international stage. This has enabled the country's economy to boom. However, this brings along its own set of problems.

In 2008, scholar Hideo Aoki pointed out that the country's economic growth had prompted "the expansion of the service economy, which has increased the life chances of the street homeless." (The service economy is an economic sector based on the buying and selling of services.)

While initially this seems like hopeful news, Aoki focused on the fact that these service jobs are often informal, unstable, and low-paying due to the economy's rapid growth. So, while there may be more jobs available, they still don't pay well enough to help homeless individuals and families off the streets. Instead, workers make just enough money off these low-paying service jobs to survive, but not enough to truly thrive.

In 2016, the country's gross domestic product increased 7.1 percent, higher than many economists' projected predictions of 6.7 percent. *Bloomberg* pointed to the nation's young population as well as the income from outsourcing as primary factors for this booming growth. However, this economic wealth is still not distributed evenly. Many poor Filipinos remain dissatisfied with their life's outlook, seeing a wide chasm between the wealthy and poor in their country.

In 2016, Rodrigo Duterte was elected president of the Philippines. During his season of election campaigns, BBC interviewed Filipinos, asking them what they were looking for in their next leader. Voters were focusing on the following election issues: the high rate of corruption, rising inequality, and the continued prevalence of poverty (still an issue even with the Philippines's strengthening economy).

Michael, a university graduate, said, "I want a new president who can create better jobs for the youth. We don't have any opportunities here."

In this country of rapid globalization, there is still a lack of opportunities for the younger demographic. Addressing the need for jobs for Manila's growing population remains a critical issue that the nation is attempting to address.

BATTLING NATURE IN THE SLUMS

In the slums of Manila, households often have crowded family trees, with at least four to five children to each set of parents. It's not uncommon for families to sleep eight to a tiny room, living in a space no bigger than a standard American bathroom.

The slums are densely populated, which means, when a natural disaster hits, thousands find themselves in danger of losing their homes. For instance, typhoons are a regular visitor to the Philippines's capital. When a typhoon floods Manila in waves, ramshackle homes in the slums are often destroyed, leaving thousands homeless. Also, the city sits on the "Ring of Fire," a name for the destructive string of volcanoes in the Pacific Ocean that often trigger huge natural disasters, such as earthquakes and tsunamis.

The waters that stream through Manila's slums are polluted to the point of toxicity.

The homes in the city's slums are often made of nothing more than sheets of plywood and bits of scrap metal. This leaves them vulnerable to the slightest spark. In February 2017, a devastating fire roared through one Manila slum, leaving more than fifteen thousand people homeless. Residents tried to curb the blaze with buckets of water, but their efforts couldn't halt the fire's progress. Firefighters who arrived on the scene struggled when they couldn't make it through the narrow alleyways that characterize Manila's slums.

In the blaze's aftermath, some homeless residents took shelter in school gymnasiums. However, many—including young teenagers—were forced to sleep on sidewalks near the burnt, demolished edges of the neighborhood they had called home.

A DANGEROUS UPBRINGING

The slums of Manila are home to thousands and thousands of young adults, all of whom are growing and developing. Here, the littered remains of dump sites served as their playgrounds growing up. Often this is where they—and their families— find their main source of food and money. They will search for scraps of food in these dump sites, while also staying on the lookout for items they can sell. This means young children

For many homeless children in Manila, garbage dumps become their living space, where they sleep and search for items to sell.

and teenagers spend a considerable amount of time foraging through these bacteria-infested sites. Sometimes, those who are forced to scavenge will wear flip-flops, but often they walk through the dump sites with bare feet.

It's also a common sight to see young children paddling up and down the polluted, blackened streams that neighbor the slums. Swimming through the water is sometimes a means of escape for the kids, though combing the river beds is another way for them to find helpful items to sell. If you visit Manila's slums and stand alongside the water—breathing in the stream's foul fumes—you can easily sense the danger of living so close to these toxic waters.

Sewage facilities are nonexistent in Manila's slums. For people living here, as well as individuals who are homeless, washing up "properly" often means paying 15 to 20 pesos (30 to 40 cents) to use a restroom in a public market. If those options aren't available, open defecation is practiced. Human waste is then tossed into the waters, which inevitably leads to the spread of bacteria and an increase in the toxicity of the water.

Growing up in these conditions is frequently detrimental to the health and well-being of young children and teenagers. Infectious diseases, like tuberculosis, filariasis, and diarrhea, are all too common in the slums of Manila. The spread of disease is quick and fast, while the potential for infection is only a small cut away.

INADEQUATE NUTRITION

While living in Manila's slums comes with the above list of potential dangers, the first and foremost concern each resident must face is how to feed themselves and their family. In these regions, many lack the funds and resources to feed every hungry mouth in their household.

Young children and teenagers in the slums often suffer from **malnutrition**, which occurs when your body does not receive the proper nutrients to grow healthy and strong. In the Food and Nutrition Research Institute's 2015 survey, they discovered that the chronic malnutrition rate for Filipino children between zero to two years of age was 26.2 percent, the highest it had been in ten years. This has the potential for serious, irreversible damage for suffering children under the age of two.

For teenagers living in the slums and those who are homeless in Manila, proper nutrition is not a luxury they can afford. This adversely affects not only their physical health, but their mental health as well.

Not having enough to eat is an indicator of severe poverty. Manila's slums are an especially impoverished area, with many living below the **poverty line** (the minimum level of income needed for someone to have enough food and water to survive). In 2012, the Philippines's poverty incidence (the number of people living under the poverty line) was recorded at 25.2 percent across the country. That number did decrease in 2015, going down to 21.6 percent. However, this number is still an alarming statistic, especially considering the economic growth of the Philippines.

According to the Philippine Statistics Authority, the minimum monthly income needed to just feed a family of five was PhP 6,329, which translates to $125.79 per month. This number does not account for other living necessities, such as a warm shelter and health services. This means 21.6 percent of the population has an income lower than $125.79 per month, even if they are pooling their family's resources together. And remember, if an individual or family is not making enough money to eat, they also likely do not have access to a proper shelter and home.

HOMELESSNESS'S ROOTS IN POVERTY

There are myriad reasons why an individual or family ends up homeless, but studies have shown that homelessness often traces back to one over-powering root cause: poverty. Poverty refers to the state of being extremely poor, to the point that affording enough food and warm shelter is next to impossible. When a family is barely making ends meet, a protective shelter is simply unaffordable.

The cycle of poverty is a stifling pattern for many families. Breaking that cycle is a crucial part of addressing homelessness.

This is certainly the case for the high number of people trying to make a living in Manila's slums. Many are stuck and rooted in a cycle of poverty. Plan International defines the concept as a cycle that begins when a child is born into a low-income family. When a family lacks funds and resources, their children have restricted access to food, safe water, safe health care, and proper schooling. This leads to hunger, poor sanitation, and a lack of education, which then increases their chances of contracting a disease and suffering from malnutrition. Faced with these debilitating circumstances, children and teenagers caught in this cycle of poverty have fewer work opportunities and repeating unemployment issues. This inevitably leads to their own low family income, which continues to create poverty in an endless, suffocating loop.

Many homeless teens of Manila begin their lives already caught in this cycle of poverty. Since their family's income is low, their health suffers and the opportunities available to them plummet. Exact statistics are hard to discover in urban Manila; however, researchers estimate anywhere between thirty thousand to seventy thousand homeless youth are living on the city's streets. The circumstances of homeless teenagers vary. While every homeless teenager in Manila faces their own set of worries, common threads bind their stories together, starting with the vulnerability of their respective lives.

A HOMELESS LIFE IN A HOMELESS FAMILY

Some homeless teenagers in Manila still have a familial support system. They are living on the streets because their entire family is homeless as well.

In 2010, UNICEF interviewed several homeless Filipino teenagers based in Manila. Thirteen-year-old Mary (a pseudonym) spoke about her life on the streets with her family. They had a house in Cavite City, but there were a slim number of opportunities to make money there. Instead, the family moved

Manila is a maze of congested streets, where too many families are living without safe, permanent shelter.

to the capital. They had a corner of sidewalk that hosted their "living" space for sleeping, cooking, and eating, located outside of a Starbucks in Binondo Square.

Her family's sidewalk corner was only available when the Starbucks employees had finally clocked out for the day. Mary said, "We don't get to sleep until after midnight."

For the thirteen-year-old, life was busy. "In the mornings I help my mother out," she said. "After waking we tidy up, then I boil some water. After that I go with Mama to buy her wares. Then I take care of my younger sister." Mary had been out of school for three years at that point. "The main problems for me are not having a place to stay and not being able to go to school," she said. "I used to go to school even when we lived on the streets, but one day when I was in the third grade, I asked Mama to go with me to school to claim my report card," she said.

"I had no idea that my little sister would go missing that day. When we returned home, she was gone. She was missing for four days until she was found by a social worker. It turns out that two kids took her while we were away … After that, my stepfather wouldn't let me go school anymore."

Mary's story speaks to the family obligations many young homeless Filipino teenagers have. Their families are struggling to get by, and all hands need to be working to ensure survival. Every single person in Mary's family had a role in helping the family survive.

"My mother works as a street vendor, selling cigarettes, snacks, and newspapers," Mary said. "My stepfather is a community guard and my older brother drives a pedicab. My younger brother Jun-jun is a jeepney barker—he hails buses and taxis for passengers." Mary's job was to help her mom and take care of her sister.

At the time, Mary was participating in street education sessions. These sessions were helping her dream of a brighter future, one where she could perhaps obtain a higher-paying job. She remarked, "Everyone has a dream and street children are no different."

Many homeless youth in the Philippines do not attend school. Yet some are able to attend education sessions hosted by social workers.

RUNNING AWAY

While some homeless teenagers live on the streets alongside their parents and siblings like Mary, others have been abandoned or have run away from a terrifying domestic situation. These homeless teenagers are forced to fend for themselves and figure out how to make a living on the streets alone, leaving them particularly vulnerable.

Manila's homeless teenagers often make a living begging for a few pesos or scavenging for saleable items they can then peddle. They might wash cars or offer to clean a stranger's shoes. But sometimes their activities run on the wrong side of the law. When desperation sets in, some homeless teenagers will engage in pick-pocketing or snatch purses. Some gamble, while others participate in high-risk activities, such as joining a gang for protection.

Child Hope Asia Philippines is a nongovernmental organization that focuses on helping homeless children and teenagers. In their resources, they emphasize the potential psychological damage for teenagers living on the streets. Life on the streets is incredibly uncertain, especially if you don't know if you'll have enough to eat the next day. Often, homeless teenagers must deal with overwhelming feelings of fear and insecurity with no support system.

Family problems often play a role in why homeless teenagers are trying to make it on their own in Manila. Another UNICEF interview conducted in 2010 was with a Filipino boy they called Cristano. He was fifteen years old at the time and had been given refuge in a youth shelter. However, prior to his change in circumstances, he had lived on the streets, having chosen to leave his violent home life. Cristano recounted:

We were very poor and my parents were always fighting. When my father got drunk, he would hit me. It started when I was six years old. He did it just because he felt like it—he wasn't himself when he was drunk. That's when I began thinking I was nothing more than a burden. A few years later I decided to run away.

After that I lived in Sangandaan Cemetery. It was very dangerous. I was in a gang … The gang would steal things like mobile phones and we would scavenge for plastic bottles and electric wire. We would sell recyclable materials to junk shops to get money for food or drugs.

I got into a lot of fights back then and I would get chased by policemen. I would get dizzy from hunger and sick with eye infections. I couldn't afford to buy any medicine when I was sick. I would beg for drinks from canteens and wash in the public toilets. Studying didn't even cross my mind. I didn't know I could go to school.

Many young teenagers living on Manila's streets are running from similarly abusive situations and end up in equally dangerous circumstances. For them, anywhere initially seems better than home. They often camp out in the corners of cemeteries or on slivers of sidewalk, trying to stay out of the way while finding enough food to eat.

On the streets of Manila, homeless people are sometimes called *yagit*, which translates to "floating garbage." This awful term is the kind of word that begins to misinform a person's identity. This abusive "nickname" damages a homeless teenager's concept of their self-worth, while also decreasing the youth's sense of community belonging.

Many homeless teenagers, like Cristano, internalize the idea that they are an unwanted burden, worth no more than the garbage they collect. This leads them to accept poorer treatment, while also believing less of their capabilities.

WANTED: OPPORTUNITIES

The homeless teenagers of Manila are missing more than a roof over their heads. They are also missing crucial opportunities that could help them build a healthier, more stable life. Some homeless teenagers have the chance to attend street education sessions, like Mary, which are run by charity organizations. This gives them the opportunity to learn and develop new skills, which is crucial to building a brighter future for homeless teenagers.

Many researchers argue that the key to breaking the cycle of poverty is to offer pathways that branch off this circular route. One effective way to help those who live in poverty is to help them get an education or receive job training. This strengthens their ability to create—and maintain—a stable, sustainable life off the streets.

MEET RODALLIE MOSENDE

In April 2016, Rodallie Mosende graduated from the Lyceum of the Philippines University with a degree in International Hospitality Management. Rodallie, like many other graduates, studied hard so she could walk across the stage to receive her diploma. The reason Rodallie's story made headlines is because she has also been homeless nearly her entire life.

Rodallie and her mother lived on the sidewalks of Paterno Street, Quiapo, Manila. As a young teenager, Rodallie begged for

Rodallie Mosende overcame homelessness to graduate from the Lyceum of the Philippines University.

food, while asking vendors to spare her family a few vegetables, promising to repay them when she could.

But Rodallie had a dream. She wanted to finish high school—and was determined to make this dream a reality. In 2011, she met Rick Rocamora, a documentary photographer who was chronicling the lives of the homeless in Quiapo. When they met, Rick was struck by Rodallie's dedication to her education. He took her picture and shared her story on social media. The tale of a homeless teenager attending a Manila high school grew viral wings. Hundreds were inspired by Rodallie's **tenacity**.

Living on the streets, Rodallie had to develop a skill set and study regime that varied from her classmates'. She learned to read by streetlight and relied on libraries to write and print papers. While in school, she continued to work as a street sweeper to pay for her food and transportation. "In our place in Quiapo, nearly all young people have lost their way," she said. "I know we have a hard life, and that's why I wanted to finish school … Sleeping on the street urged me to try my best to leave."

The photographs of Rodallie cast a spotlight on her situation. Many wanted to lend a helping hand. An anonymous benefactor offered her a scholarship to attend university, and others donated to fund her secondary school dreams as well. While many news stories focused on her hard-working dedication, it's important to note Rodallie was also afforded the opportunity to continue her secondary education thanks to her benefactor. Since her graduation from university, she now has a skill set that will allow her to invest in a future working in the hospitality industry.

Rodallie has stated that what homeless teenagers want most is to regain a sense of human dignity. They don't want to be treated as inferior, but rather as an equal and important member of their community. This valuing of youth would go a long way in changing how homeless teenagers are perceived, as well begin making room for real and important change to their access to education, health services, and more.

Rick, the documentary photographer who brought Rodallie's story to the international stage, said, "[Rodallie's] story, especially with a benefactor giving her a college scholarship, can uniquely show how an act from someone can make a difference to someone's life." Rick stated we have a shared "responsibility of raising educated children," which would help more homeless children and teenagers step out of the cycle of poverty.

Plan International defined the cycle of poverty as being circular—and potentially set to continually repeat. But there's a clear answer to solve this persistent problem. One of the best ways to fight poverty, a major root cause of homelessness, is to begin investing in the children and teenagers who are on the streets. You only need to look at Rodallie's story—and her hopeful future—to see the difference this investment would make.

A DAY IN ALVARO'S LIFE

In 2014, a staff reporter from the *Toronto Star* met Alvaro, then sixteen years old, who was living on the streets of Manila. Alvaro's story gives a glimpse into the day-to-day life of a young, homeless Filipino boy trying to survive and be happy.

Alvaro was used to being homeless. He slept on the grounds of Plaza Salamanca, a partially shaded park seemingly made of concrete, where many homeless youth spend their nights. As soon as the sun rose, right until the sun set, Alvaro would do his day job—asking for money from drivers waiting in Manila's traffic jams. His feet pounded the pavement in flip-flops, as he knocked on windows, trying to encourage drivers to spare him a few pesos.

This line of work would maybe net him about thirty pesos a day. In American change, this barely adds up to sixty cents. Earning thirty pesos meant he could afford a bowl of rice in the morning but perhaps not another bowl at night. Alvaro also spent time sifting through garbage, hoping to find a banana slice or a piece of mango to assuage his hunger.

In the evening, Alvaro took a break from his life's endless cycle of begging, scavenging, asking, and hoping. He would go sing karaoke. In the Philippines, karaoke is more than a national pastime—it's a way of life. There's a karaoke machine in nearly every household, and it is a Filipino inventor who holds the patent for the first Karaoke Sing-Along System.

For Alvaro, the music provided an escape from the fear and uncertainty that plagued his life on the streets. His musical stage was Laura's Kitchen, a combined bar and restaurant just down the road from Plaza Salamanca. He would go with five other friends, each one graciously taking a turn to sing. The karaoke machines charged five pesos (ten cents) per song. Each teenager barely glanced at the lyric prompter because they were so sure of the words.

Song choices among the boys ranged from Bruno Mars to Celine Dion and from Katy Perry to more traditional, local songs. At the time, his friend sang "Anak," a love song sung in Tagalog. That day, Alvaro chose Air Supply's "The One That You Love" to sing, belting out the song with dedicated devotion.

"What do I dream?" he said. "I dream what we all dream, to be the next Arnel Pineda."

Pineda is a Filipino singer and local legend, who makes a living off his smooth serenading abilities. The singer was discovered on YouTube. This led to Pineda lining up his biggest gig to date as the lead singer for the rock band Journey. Now, Pineda has international fame and recognition. Alvaro hoped for the same kind of success.

During the day, Alvaro was stuck, occasionally watching customers exit the Wendy's restaurant nearby, dreaming of better food and a stable life. But, at night, his dreams expanded when the music swelled, as he hoped for a promising future filled with song.

CHAPTER THREE

Homeless Teens in New York City

New York City—also colloquially known as the Empire City, the Big Apple, and the City that Never Sleeps— truly has a mammoth global reputation. There are few cities worldwide that boast the same catalogue of iconic landmarks and international prestige. The city is also steeped in history, widely remembered—and still seen—as a gateway into the United States. New York City was and is an entry point to America (and the American dream), which has solidified its reputation as a city for dreamers of new beginnings.

New York City is a city with a robust economy, and many of its citizens carry equally robust wallets. There is a tide of wealth that runs through the many expensive avenues of Manhattan, and it's easy to suppose that in a city so well-off that there must be very few people who go to bed hungry. Yet, New York City, the shining "Financial Hub" of America, has one of the country's largest homeless populations—and the city is struggling mightily to house them all.

Opposite: New York City has one of America's largest homeless populations.

CALLAHAN V. CAREY

New York City has a unique tactic for addressing homelessness in its neighborhoods. New York state is one of the only American states where it is a legal right for all homeless individuals and families to have access to shelter.

This landmark decision was the result of a class action lawsuit filed in 1979 against the city of New York. Robert Hayes, a lawyer and co-founder of the Coalition for the Homeless, launched the class action lawsuit, arguing that it was (and is) a constitutional state right for all in need to have access to shelter. The lawsuit highlighted Article XVII of the New York State Constitution, which notes that "the aid, care and support of the needy are public concerns and shall be provided by the state and by such of its subdivisions ..."

In August 1981, following back-and-forth negotiations, *Callahan v. Carey* was finally settled. The city and state would begin providing shelter to all homeless individuals who met "the need standard for welfare or who were homeless 'by reason of physical, mental, or social dysfunction.'" Not only did the settlement require all homeless individuals be provided shelter, it also mandated that the shelters had to meet basic health and safety standards.

However, New York City's "legal right to shelter" is not without its complications. While on the surface this would appear to address homelessness in an effective manner, the implementation of this policy has not always been successful—especially when it comes to homeless youth. In recent years, homelessness has been on the rise in New York City, and the city is struggling to find enough accommodation for everyone. The rising homeless statistics begs the question: Does the city need to strengthen its strategy to combat homelessness?

The decision in the lawsuit *Callahan v. Carey* found that everyone has a right to shelter. Homeless shelters in New York are required to provide clean clothes and safe beds.

CLIMBING NUMBERS

In December 2016, there were 62,674 people in New York City without shelter. According to New York City's Coalition for the Homeless, this number registers as one of the highest since the Great Depression of the 1930s. The primary reason cited is the lack of affordable housing, a rising concern in this city full of high-priced apartments. According to the Coalition for the Homeless, other major triggers that lead to homelessness in New York include "eviction, doubled-up or severely overcrowded housing, domestic violence, job loss, and hazardous housing conditions."

Some experts claim New York City is facing a homelessness epidemic. The city is scrambling to address this issue in a meaningful manner. In 2016, the city's mayor, Bill de Blasio, spent $1.6 billion on building solutions to help the homeless of the city. This cache of money is 60 percent more than what de Blasio spent previously to help the city's homeless population when he first became mayor in January 2014.

While New York City remains one of the few American cities with a legal right to shelter (thanks to the lawsuit *Callahan v. Carey*), the solutions found are not always ideal. And the ones who are often left out in the cold are the teenagers who are caught between youth and adulthood.

NEW YORK'S YOUTH HOMELESSNESS CRISIS

In New York City, the number of homeless teenagers between the ages of sixteen to twenty is estimated to hover around the 3,800 mark. But it is frustratingly difficult to compile accurate totals. Homeless youth in the Big Apple—and in many other

In Brooklyn, a homeless teenager settles in to sleep on a park bench.

American cities—have mastered the art of blending in. They are often invisible to the public eye, looking the spitting image of an **affluent** teen in the city—until you look closely.

You can spot New York's homeless teenagers in specific haunts around the city. Some catch precious minutes of rest when they ride with "Uncle A.C.E.," a nickname for the longest subway route. Others charge their phones while they sit in bus terminals, looking like any other teenager waiting to go home to a warm bed. Quite a few are **couch surfers**, who move from one friend's apartment to another. Many will linger at twenty-four-hour McDonald's and other fast food restaurants, buying cheap meals in exchange for a place to sit and rest for as long as they can.

Of course there are many reasons for teen homelessness in New York City, but there's one in particular: there are not enough specialized shelter beds for teenagers. Before 2016, the city had only 453 beds for youth between the ages of sixteen to twenty. Half of those 453 beds were **crisis beds**, strictly for short-term residencies. Crisis beds offer emergency shelter but only allow stays of up to sixty days. Essentially, there were 453 beds for a homeless youth population that is counted in the thousands. It's not surprising that most of the city's youth-oriented shelters had (and still have) waiting lists.

Youth-oriented shelters, such as Covenant House, are rare in New York City.

Part of the reason there is lack of youth-oriented shelter beds is because the city believes older teenagers (those who are eighteen years old and up) can turn to adult shelters for housing instead. For many young homeless youth, adult shelters are an unwelcoming, scary place to call home. The crowds at the adult shelters are quite a bit older, and teenagers are often harassed. So, teenagers without shelter in New York turn to other avenues. Instead of seeking a shelter, they wind up on the streets, in McDonald's, and on subways, trying to find spaces to sleep peacefully.

In recent years, **advocates** have begun fighting this specific issue, including the Legal Aid Society. In December 2013, the Legal Aid Society filed a federal lawsuit on behalf of New York City's homeless youth in their late teens. Their lawsuit is fighting for the rights of the city's 3,800 homeless youth (sixteen to twenty years of age), demanding that each one should have access to shelters and services that will serve their needs as young teenagers.

Beth Hofmeister, staff attorney in the Homeless Rights Projects, has said, "The reasons that runaway and homeless youth become homeless are different from the reasons that single adults become homeless or families become homeless." And, since the reasons are different, this also means their needs are different. However, the needs of homeless teenagers can only be properly addressed in a youth-oriented environment. Shuffling them into an adult shelter is not a long-term solution.

In January 2016, de Blasio announced the city's plan to add 300 extra beds for youth ages sixteen to twenty, driving the total up to 753 beds. This has been viewed as a welcome step forward—albeit still falling short of how many additional beds are truly needed. The homeless population of New York City is still growing and stronger policy changes need to be on the horizon.

Kim Forte, one of the Legal Aid Society's attorneys behind the federal lawsuit, can see the possibilities of a future where youth-oriented resources are available to homeless teenagers:

New York is in a great position to tackle homeless youth issues. It has one of the largest homeless youth populations in the country, [and] it certainly has the means and resources to set up a continuum of care so that young people who are homeless, independent of their families, can be treated like young people and can receive supportive services such that we can decrease the number. What we know to be true is that if they exist, homeless youth resources and shelter actually work.

THE EXPERIENCES OF
LGBTQIA+ HOMELESS TEENAGERS

Debates continue over whether the homeless youth population of New York City and other American cities are underserved. The consensus generally agrees more could be done. But perhaps where the most additional help is needed is addressing the specific experiences of one particularly vulnerable group of homeless teenagers: those who identify as part of the LGBTQIA+ community.

It is estimated that nearly half of the homeless teenagers in America are part of the LGBTQIA+ community.

In 2014, the Williams Institute released their national survey of service providers working with homeless youth. These service providers included drop-in centers, street outreach programs, and housing programs. The Williams Institute's survey dug up some surprising numbers. They discovered 30 to 43 percent of the homeless youth who interacted with these service providers identified as LGBTQIA+.

This is a massive percentage, nearly covering half of the total population of homeless teenagers. The survey also released additional statistics, ranking the top five reasons why LGBTQIA+ youth were homeless or at-risk of becoming homeless: 46 percent "ran away because of family rejection of [their] sexual orientation or gender identity," 43 percent were "forced out by parents because of sexual orientation or gender identity," 32 percent faced "physical, emotional, or sexual abuse at home," 17 percent had "aged out of the foster care system," and 14 percent had suffered "financial or emotional neglect from family."

These reasons point to a troublesome trend: most LGBTQIA+ homeless youth are without shelter due to their family's rejection of their sexual orientation and/or gender identity. While progress has been made in the fairness and equality of treatment of the LGBTQIA+ community, these statistics are a disheartening look at the discrimination still faced by young teenagers who identify as part of the LGBTQIA+ community. This discrimination and rejection leads to many LGBTQIA+ struggling to find safe shelter.

In a 2015 *Advocate* article, Carl Siciliano, the founder of the Ali Forney Center (a center dedicated to protecting the rights of LGBTQIA+ homeless youth), compiled stories from the teenagers he'd worked with who'd lived on the streets. The teenagers, all who identified as part of the LGBTQIA+ community, talked of their feelings of exclusion and fear, major stressors that tampered with their overall well-being.

Angel, then twenty-two, told his story:

My grandmother raised me and my brothers and sisters. She died when I was fourteen. For a while I stayed with

"It was better when I stayed in an LGBT shelter," said Angel. "They respected me when I was transitioning."

my aunt. It was a nightmare. She wouldn't recognize my gender. I had a job at a theater, and she charged me $200 a week to sleep in a clothes closet on a pillow. I tried to make the best of it …

When I became homeless I tried to go to a big shelter for hundreds of kids. The intake worker refused to respect my gender identity. I showed her that I had a male ID, but she said it didn't make a difference …

They put me in a female dorm. One of the other girls there said I couldn't use the bathroom unless I [paid] her $40! She raised her fist to me and threatened me for $40! I couldn't deal with it, so I decided to sleep in the subway. I slept in the subway for two weeks. I found the whole thing so stressful that I couldn't eat.

Quincy, then twenty-one, also shared his experiences:

I had to leave my home because my mother couldn't accept me. She would get angry about the way I acted and the clothes I wore ...

For a while after I left home I was sleeping on friends' couches. Then for two weeks straight I was sleeping on the subway. I would clutch all my stuff really tight, holding them close, especially after I was robbed.

Mornings were rough because I was so exhausted. I could never get enough sleep, only two or three hours. It took a toll on my body. I was always tired and irritated. I couldn't focus.

I was afraid to go to the men's shelter. I have a friend who stayed there, and when they found out he was gay they beat him up mercilessly. If they would do that to a grown man, what would they do to a scrawny twenty-one-year-old gay kid.

When you are on the streets, riding the subways, nights are very tough. Sometimes I felt so alone. Nobody cared, nobody asked about me. I was just alone.

As always, it bears mentioning that every homeless youth has their own story and experiences. One teenager's experience does not encompass them all. But Angel and Quincy's stories offer insight into the specific despairs and troubles of LGBTQIA+ youth who are living on the streets. Many are struggling to survive in hostile environments that remain unaccepting of their sexual orientations and/or gender identities. Learning to accept and understand who you are is difficult enough when you're a teenager. LGBTQIA+ teenagers who are homeless are also dealing with the boundaries of hostile living environments. They are targeted and misunderstood.

For homeless teenagers, a shelter should provide more than a warm bed. It also should be a safe space, and for LGBTQIA+ homeless youth, finding these safe spaces can seem impossible. And, when finding shelter seems futile, many turn to a desperate measure: prostitution. It's named **survival sex**, and according to a 2015 *Urban Institute* study, LGBTQIA+ homeless youth were seven to eight times more than likely than their cisgender, heterosexual peers to have traded sex for money or shelter. Studies have shown that LGBTQIA+ homeless youth are much more likely to engage in survival sex to avoid the alternative: youth or adult shelters, where their neighbors are likely to be violently hostile toward a member of the LGBTQIA+ community.

Survival sex can look like the only way for homeless teenagers to generate an income, especially if they're part of the LGBTQIA+ community. Finding a job when you're homeless and a teenager is a steep hill to climb. To begin with, lacking a stable shelter makes it incredibly difficult to hold down a regular job. If you're constantly on the move, you often can't get to work on time or get enough sleep to function properly at your job. Furthermore, many LGBTQIA+ homeless youth face often face discrimination on the job market due to their appearance, sexual orientation, and/or gender identity. This is another complication that decreases their chances of finding a stable job to fund a life off the streets. Too often for LGBTQIA+ homeless youth, survival sex seems the only "solution."

A 2012 *New York Times* op-ed featured a brief interview with Donna, a transgender woman who turned to prostitution at the age of thirteen. She said, "People call you a survivor after you leave the life. But I was a survivor when I was in it. I didn't really like prostituting. But then, I had no other way out."

RESILIENT, IN SPITE OF IT ALL

While the singular struggles of homeless teenagers should be acknowledged—and, more importantly, understood—it's crucial to not paint them as victims. Labeling homeless youth as victims of the streets undermines the resourcefulness and resilience of those who find themselves growing up very quickly in an uncompromising world.

Sean A. Kidd and Larry Davidson's 2007 study, "'You Have to Adapt Because You Have No Other Choice': The Stories of Strength and Resilience of 208 Homeless Youth in New York City and Toronto," tracked the narratives of more than two hundred homeless teenagers. The researchers sought to answer these two questions: "How do [homeless teenagers] make it out here? How do they survive?" Common themes emerged in the answers they heard.

On the streets, the teenagers interviewed often had no one to rely on. One interviewee said, "At home you are sheltered. You've got your mom and your dad or whatever. Out here it is just you. You learn a lot of independence."

To survive living on the streets, the teenagers built upon the strength they found within themselves. A second interviewee said, "The street, it helped me to be strong. Don't let nobody hurt you. I used to be really sensitive. I had to get strong because there are people who try to hurt you out there. They treat you like a piece of garbage and you have to get some strength."

A third interviewee disclosed, "You have to adapt … even for the wrong reasons. You have to adapt out of convenience. You have to adapt to get what you want. You have to adapt because you have no other choice."

Kidd, who conducted the interviews, notes that his discussions with homeless teenagers yielded "narratives of young people struggling to understand their lives, possibly a greater struggle than most because of their marginalized and often extremely challenging circumstances. It is a struggle for definition and valuing of self, for a sense of meaningful life, and for connection with others."

The homeless teenagers of New York City, especially those who are part of the LGBTQIA+ community, are facing incomprehensible struggles. But their stories encompass more than their struggles. Their stories are also filled with humanity, the real lives of young people who are still building their identities and making a life lifted on their own two shoulders. Their stories should be a call to action. They should inspire the creation of more safe spaces for teenagers, no matter their age, sexual orientation, and/or gender identity. Their stories remind us we can dream of a New York City—and an America—where every homeless teenager has the option of safe, secure, and welcoming shelter. And it's a dream that is hopefully on its way to becoming a reality—however slowly that may be.

SAMANTHA'S STORY

Samantha Green (a pseudonym), an LGBTQIA+ teen, was the subject of a 2012 *New Yorker* profile. It was early September 2009 when Samantha left her Florida hometown. She left behind—with no regrets—a set of parents who refused to believe her when she told them of a relative's sexual assault. Samantha needed to leave her toxic home environment behind, so she set her eyes on New York City. Her vision for the future was squarely set in the city for dreamers, where she believed the building blocks for a new life could be found.

Samantha had been crafting her escape route for months. She'd always gotten straight As, imagining a life unfurling on a college campus. But tuition fees held that dream back, so Samantha changed the setting of her dreams: she was going to New York City for a new life.

The summer of 2009 was a time of planning for Samantha. She knew she wouldn't have the funds to rent an apartment in the city, so she spent hours researching the "how" of homelessness in New York City. She built a guide for her future life on the streets, listing soup kitchens (for meals), recreation centers (for showers), and bottle-return stations (for money). The guide was bundled into a purple spiral notebook.

Samantha spent her first days in Central Park, still only seventeen years old. She knew that if she went to a shelter, they would be legally obligated to call her parents. So she slept on benches, cradling an open book in her arms, trying to match the appearance of a student who had accidentally fallen asleep in the park. Her sleep patterns never veered into a deep REM cycle, her ears constantly on the lookout for footsteps and police radios.

She spent days mapping the city, watching how the neighborhoods of New York City lit up and when its citizens woke up. She discovered that the Museum of Natural History had narrow bathroom stalls, perfect for a light nap with her head against the stall sides.

To make friends in the homeless youth community, she shared cigarettes. She learned how to spot the other homeless teenagers, many of whom whiled away their days at the Apple Store on Fifth Avenue. The teenagers would hover around the cheaper computers, likely wearing the one trendy outfit they had, which they'd have stolen previously. Samantha handed out her résumé to fast food shop after fast food shop, but her appearance (she only had one set of clothes) and her lack of work experience meant there were never follow-up calls. Bottle recycling was the work domain of the older homeless crowd. Left with no alternatives, she shoplifted.

At the time, Samantha tracked the stolen merchandise, convinced she could pay the vendors back in the future. Regarding this belief, she later wrote, "I now know that's impossible."

Then, Samantha finally turned eighteen. She wore a shoestring as a belt to hold up pants that were looser due to a month with little food. She entered a shelter for the first time. And so, the next chapter of Samantha's life as a homeless teenager in New York City began.

Homeless teen Samantha spent her first days (and nights) after arriving in New York City in Central Park.

CHAPTER FOUR

Homeless Teens in Nairobi

N airobi, the capital of Kenya, is nicknamed the "Green City in the Sun," an apt description for a city that is regularly bathed in sunlight. The city's day-to-day temperatures hover in the 70s and 80s (21.1 to 26.6 degrees Celsius), a sunny environment for Nairobi's array of wildlife. The city is a common entry point for tourists and businessmen alike, and the cosmopolitan capital is known as the beating heart of its country. It is also home to over 3.1 million people who must contend with the urban intensity of Nairobi.

Nairobi's population, much like Manila's, has skyrocketed over the last few decades. The last official census in 2009 totaled up to double the city's population in 1986. This massive population growth is largely due to the migration of Kenya's rural residents to big cities in search of employment. This is a budding trend not just in Kenya, but throughout the entirety of Africa.

Opposite: Nairobi is the thriving cornerstone of Kenya, yet the city struggles to address the needs of its homeless population.

Kenya has a population of over forty-six million people. Astonishingly, more than 40 percent of the country's population is under the age of fifteen. This youthful set of citizens places immense pressure on the Kenya's job market—a worrisome issue, especially in Nairobi.

Nairobi shares other similarities with Manila, namely its rapidly developing globalism. Many international companies are attempting to gain a foothold in Nairobi, and this has given Kenya's capital an international flavor. But, as with Manila, this rapid growth has produced a towering population in a city that lacks the infrastructure to care for everyone adequately—especially when it comes to the homeless youth who are tucked away and ignored on the streets of Nairobi.

Experts estimate that there are between 250,000 to 300,000 homeless youth living on the streets in Kenya. Sixty thousand of the country's homeless teenagers—approximately 20 percent of all Kenyan youth without shelter—are living in Nairobi. And, for a city known for basking in the sun's spotlight, Nairobi's population of homeless teenagers often live in the shadows.

MARGINALIZED AND BATTLING ADDICTION

In *IRIN*'s 2017 "Youth in Crisis: Coming of age in the 21st century," fifteen-year-old William, a homeless teenager in Nairobi, stated:

> I lost my parents three years ago and since then I have been living in the streets without shelter and assurance of having food every day. Nobody cares about me; whether I live or not. People don't want to look at me.

For many Kenyan youth, living on the streets is their only option for survival. This leaves them exceedingly vulnerable.

I'm trash. I don't want to live in the streets, but I have nobody. My uncle beat me hard when I lived there, and so I ran. Living in the streets is the only way to survive.

William's despair, coupled with his rejection from his surrounding community, is all too common among homeless teenagers. Young adults without permanent shelter are constantly battling an overwhelming set of feelings. On a day-to-day basis, they deal with hunger, fear, exhaustion, cold, loneliness, a lack of self-worth, and anxiety. Most must manage this mixture of emotions without a support network and with limited access to mental health resources. And, in Nairobi and its surrounding areas, access to supportive resources are even scarcer for homeless teenagers. However, here, there is one readily available substance that many use to cope with life on the streets: industrial glue.

According to the National Institute on Drug Abuse, inhalants (like industrial glue) "produce a rapid high that resembles alcohol intoxication, with initial excitation followed by drowsiness, disinhibition, lightheadedness, and agitation." Taken long-term, inhalants are tough for users to quit, which prompts "compulsive use."

In Nairobi and its surrounding areas, industrial glue has a stronghold on the drug scene, especially on the streets. For most homeless teenagers, the industrial glue is too expensive to purchase from a vendor. However, *mama pimas* (middle men) purchase the glue, whittling the full amount into smaller plastic bottles. The smaller quantities are then sold for about twenty-five cents per bottle. The glue is often cheaper than food, and a few sniffs will buoy the user for several hours.

In Kenya, industrial glue is not a controlled substance. This, combined with its wide availability, make the drug very easy for anyone to obtain and use. When living in an environment where resources are scarce, this addictive glue appears to provide a path toward survival—albeit a very dangerous one. For the homeless teenagers of Nairobi and its surrounding areas, sniffing glue helps them combat the cold, making them feel warmer, while numbing the endless hunger pangs. This numbness helps them complete more difficult labor for cash on the side, while also helping them to forget their problems temporarily. For some, sniffing industrial glue makes them feel bolder and braver, emotions that can be fleeting but feel necessary to survive in the harsh reality of the streets.

The glue provides escape for many of the homeless teenagers in Nairobi, though at an extremely high cost. Studies have shown that many of the teenagers who are addicted to glue have no idea of drug's level of harm. They moderately understand how the drug adversely affects their health. Many who sniff glue end up suffering stomach and knee pains. But their level of addiction is often too high for them to consider stopping.

Instead, the immediacy of their survival instincts pushes them down the dangerous path of sniffing glue. It's a nearly impossible struggle to let this drug go, and many homeless teenagers in Nairobi believe that their body is too addicted to ever fully stop.

Most of Nairobi's homeless teenagers begin sniffing glue to feel a part of their "street family." They feel a certain amount of pressure to follow their peers' leads. Friends who are homeless together will typically sniff glue together, and the drug has since become an outlet for connection.

In one study in Eldoret, Kenya, 91 percent of the interviewed Kenyan street youth wished there were services that could help them kick their glue addiction. About 93 percent also felt that their community could be helping them curb the habit. Unfortunately, there are few government or charity programs that address this particular concern on the streets.

The glue addiction of homeless teenagers in Nairobi and surrounding areas unfortunately feeds into the negative public perception of their plight. The homeless youth who are addicted to sniffing industrial glue are viewed as outcasts and non-contributors to the wider community.

"When people see some of these kids, they do not take them as human beings," said Moha, a former homeless teenager in Nairobi, who was quoted in the *Daily Nation*. "When people see them sniffing glue and dirty, they beat them or insult them … It is quite difficult to describe the situation … you find if they sleep outside someone's shop, in the morning, instead of the owner waking them up gently, they kick them or even pour water on them."

Sniffing glue induces drowsiness, and some of Nairobi's homeless teenagers lie on the streets, high on the intoxication of the inhalant. Many within the wider Kenyan community point to these images as evidence of laziness among the street's young adults. But that surface-level accusation misses the nuances of the issue. It also ignores the desire of many homeless teenagers to end their addiction to inhalants—but who are unable to do so without proper help and resources.

PEER SUPPORT AND WORK ETHIC

In many ways, the place you call "home" informs your identity. The roof over your head provides protection from the elements, but it also gives you a sense of safety and belonging within your community. When a teenager lacks a permanent, safe residence, they must forfeit that sense of security and stability. A homeless

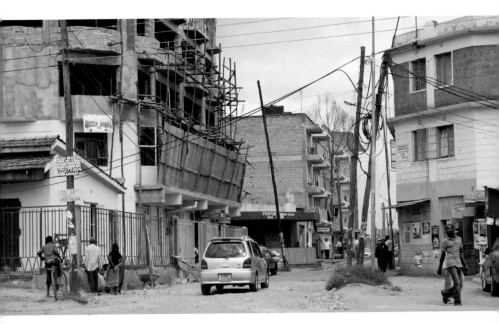

Crumbling infrastructure plagues many neighborhoods in Nairobi.

teenager often struggles to feel like they have a place where they belong, which is a feeling echoed by many of the youth living on the streets of Nairobi and its surrounding areas. To gain a sense of belonging, many homeless teenagers in Kenya instead build new families with their peers living alongside them.

"We see that the rest of the community hates us," said Joan in a 2009 CNN article, then nineteen years old and living on Nairobi's streets. "We ask ourselves if the community is not taking care of us, we should remain as our own family."

These "street families" are just as close-knit as blood relatives. They bandage each other's injuries and divide their limited resources. Work opportunities are shared among them all, and each are loyal to the peers. They look out for each other, a caring—and crucial—act in a world that isn't looking out for them.

In the 2008 *Children and Youth Services Review*'s paper, "Are street children beyond rehabilitation?," researchers analyzed the make-up of the different groups of homeless teenagers in Nakuru, a Kenyan city close to Nairobi. The researchers found there were three distinct groups of homeless teenage boys in the city: the "begging boys," the "plastic bag sellers," and the "market boys." All of them were between nine to eighteen years old.

The "begging boys" were the youngest—and, according to the researcher, the most vulnerable—as they begged for money around town. When their pockets were empty, they scoured through trash bins, hunting for leftover vegetables and fruit. The young boys slept together in groups, all wearing shabby clothes and carrying glue bottles to sniff away hunger pangs. Nearly all of them were under fifteen years of age.

The "plastic bag sellers" spent their days at the Kamkunji supermarket, which was their territory. No one except them could sell plastic bags there. Their days started early—at eight o'clock in the morning—and wound down at six o'clock in the evening. The boys all took a one-hour lunch break, eating a cheap meal of beans with rice. All the "plastic bag sellers" lived in a single room in a slum, paying 300 Kenyan shillings for the month (roughly $3 per month). The average daily wage for each seller was about 80 Kenyan shillings (about 77 cents).

Finally, the "market boys" were among the oldest of Nakuru's homeless youth, ranging in age from fifteen to eighteen. Like the "plastic bag sellers," they also worked outside of the market, but used push carts to help move heavy luggage for customers. They all went "home" to different places—some to sections of sidewalks, others in rented rooms they shared with three to four other boys. The work days of the "market boys" began even earlier than the "plastic bag sellers." Their days started at six o'clock in the morning—aiding the early morning customers—and their work wrapped up around six o'clock in the evening. They, too, would take a lunch break, eating a meal at the local soup kitchen.

The researchers observed that the group of boys all lived by their own code of ethics. The older boys of the groups would take newcomers under their wing, teaching them the "rules of working on the streets." Newcomers were given "peer support and survival skills," both crucial to making a living while on the streets. One boy said, "When you belong to a specific group, you know everything about that group. We tell each other everything and support each other in everything."

The researchers noted, "Once the boys have left their immediate families, they are sustained on the streets by peer mutual trust and friendship and depend on each other entirely for meeting day-to-day needs for work opportunities, shelter, food and healthcare." The support system of each individual group was crucial to their survival. What's also interesting to note is the **work ethic** of the groups of boys, the diligence and number of hours it took for them to make their "bare-minimum" wages.

Some experts have stated that some of Kenya's homeless teenagers could be classified as "**working poor**," a phrase that applies to workers who have jobs but whose incomes fall below their country's poverty line. This definition accounts for the work ethic of many of Kenya's homeless youth, especially groups of boys like the "plastic bag sellers" and "market boys." This also directly contradicts the overwhelming societal perception that Kenya's homeless teenagers are "lazy" and non-contributing members of their community.

Redefining our preconceived notions is one way to start change. And, in the case of Kenya's homeless teenagers, redefining their perception in society could help change their stories.

THE "INVISIBLE" GIRLS

In the above study, the researchers only focused on the homeless boys of Naruka. They had originally wanted to include girls in their study, but found it impossible. Girls were "not visible on the streets because, as [the researchers] learnt later from the boys, the girls are controlled by men for prostitution purposes."

A difficult reality faces the young, homeless women of Nairobi and its surrounding areas. Many are victims of sexual violence and live a risk-filled, harsh life on the streets. Experts estimate that approximately 25 percent of homeless teenagers in Nairobi are young women. Yet many are "invisible," even more so than their male counterparts. Young women who are homeless are understudied in academic research, which translates to fewer organizations that directly address the female concerns of the young homeless population. The female experience of homelessness shares some similarities with the male experience of homelessness, but there are crucial differences that make life more difficult for young women on the streets.

According to Joan in the 2009 CNN article, "Living in the streets, especially if you are a girl, is very risky. You can be raped any day, any time, by anyone who wants to do it." Experts agree that young homeless women are among the most vulnerable of the homeless population in Nairobi and its surrounding areas. In a 2012 *African Journal of Midwifery and Women's Health* study, "Being homeless: Reasons and challenges faced by affected women," researchers stated that homeless girls "more frequently report sexual, physical and emotional abuse, express higher rates of depression, and experience more suicide attempts than boys."

Rescue Dada, a rehabilitation center for young street girls, estimated up to 80 percent of young homeless women in Kenya face sexual abuse while living on the streets. The young women are overpowered by older and stronger men, putting them at risk of unwanted pregnancies and HIV infections.

For many young homeless women of Kenya, there is pressure on them to rely on a man's assistance. Another participant in the study, a twenty-one-year-old woman, said, "My friends told me living in the streets require one to have a man friend. In the night you do not have to sleep alone. A man will take

The "invisible" girls of Nairobi live in the shadows,
their needs often overlooked and neglected.

care of you. I was not for this idea but with time I agreed with them."

The gender "hierarchy" on Kenya's streets gives a glimpse at how difficult life is for a young homeless woman. They have limited opportunities in this world dominated and shaped by men. What is most troubling is that many of these young women feel **disempowered**, deprived of authority over their own lives.

In her interview, the twenty-one-year-old participant added, "I will be very happy if I am assisted to get out of the street. I do not mind doing any kind of job. No one wants to employ a street person. I have tried to look for house work but I have not found [any]."

HOPE FOR THE FUTURE

In Nairobi and its surrounding areas, homeless teenagers are constantly face-to-face with the **stigma** of their situation, the "mark of disgrace" regarding their homelessness. They are seen as non-contributing members of their community rather than young individuals, worthy of respect, who are facing difficult circumstances. For the homeless teenagers of Nairobi and its surrounding areas, a good first step would be for community members to recognize these teenagers' individual potential and helping them foster that potential into ability, so they can begin to build more stable lives.

GLOBAL IMPACT: REWIRING OUR SOCIETAL PERSPECTIVE ON HOMELESSNESS

Worldwide, we all lose when we approach our community's homeless populations with indifference and negativity instead of understanding and compassion. In Nairobi, the city's homeless population are labeled and treated as outcasts from their community. Unfortunately, this societal perspective on homelessness is not specific to Nairobi. A resoundingly negative outlook on homelessness in general is echoed across many communities around the globe.

Many homeless teenagers hide their living situation in fear of the sticky stigma attached to being homeless. This stigma severely hinders progress in addressing the needs of homeless teenagers in the United States and across the world. It also affects the self-esteem of homeless individuals, who feel undervalued and ignored, while slowing down policies that could instigate real change.

This is a story that needs to change. Homelessness cannot be solved with a single method, but there is a simple step forward. It's time for us to make eye contact. It's time for us to make our "invisible" homeless population visible.

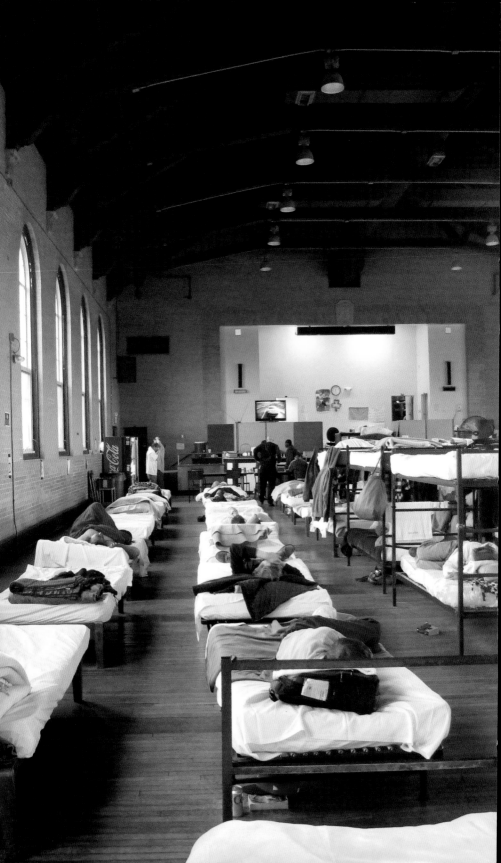

CHAPTER FIVE

Looking Ahead

Just like there is no one narrative that encompasses the experiences of all homeless teenagers, there isn't one straightforward solution to help youth who are living without a safe, permanent shelter. However, in recent years, inroads have been made in the study of homelessness. More resources are becoming available to those without shelter. And, most importantly, these resources are services and programs that address the specific needs of different groups of homeless individuals.

In our case studies, three thematic ideas were discussed. In Manila's case study, we examined poverty as one of the root causes of homelessness, while New York City's case study focused on the need to create safe spaces for homeless teenagers, especially for LGBTQIA+ youth. Nairobi's case study addressed the need

Opposite: Many shelters remain cramped spaces. Hopefully, this will change in the future with further funding and community support.

to realign the societal perception of homelessness, which is perhaps one of the strongest ways to ensure homeless teenagers are treated with fairness and dignity. Each of these overarching themes outline and define the issue of teen homelessness. This chapter takes a deeper look at how individuals and organizations are addressing these topics.

PATH BY PATH: BREAKING THE CYCLE OF POVERTY

In Manila, New York City, Nairobi, and communities around the globe, poverty remains one of the major determining factors as to why an individual or family is homeless. And the fact remains that the cycle of poverty is incredibly difficult to break.

However, recent research is crediting brain science as one way to address the cycle of poverty. According to *Crittenton Women's Union*'s "Using Brain Science to Design New Pathways Out of Poverty," poverty directly affects the brain's **executive function (EF) skills**. These include three main skills: impulse control, working memory, and mental flexibility. A person's impulse control is more than your ability to say "no" to chocolate. Your impulse control directly relates to your ability to ignore distractions, keep focus in unstable times, and to continue toward your goals despite worries you may have. Your working memory is the flexibility of your mind's labyrinth. If a person can consider many different items at once, connect the dots between various pieces of information, and follow directions with several steps, they have a strong working memory. Mental flexibility enables an individual to calibrate priorities, use different social skills in different settings, and

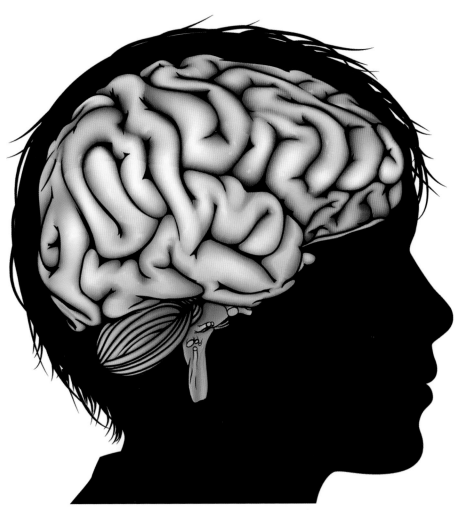

Researchers believe the strengthening of executive function (EF) skills holds the key to effectively combating poverty.

innovate in their day-to-day lives. We tend to underrate our executive function skills—or are unaware of their existence. But a person's EF skills are crucial to developing a sustainable, healthy life on their own and with their family.

When someone is living under the poverty line, like many homeless teenagers are, they are under an extraordinary amount of stress. Research has shown this directly affects their executive function skills. Essentially, the stress of poverty limits the full development of EF skills. In a 2014 *San Francisco Foundation* post, "Five Takeaways on Breaking the Cycle of Poverty," the author notes that when "executive functions are compromised ... impulses are extremely difficult to control. It's harder to calm down; dealing with authority feels threatening; maintaining confidence is challenging; and being resilient to make myriad decision[s] necessary to hold jobs ... feels impossible." In multiple, unnerving ways, the compromising of EF skills directly affects a person's ability to build a life.

Recognizing how poverty—and, in relation, homelessness—can rewire the brain is crucial to our understanding of how to break the cycle of poverty. While poverty can stress the development of an individual's EF skills, there are ways to combat the effects. Our brains have incredible plasticity, which means they can be remolded and rebuilt. This means that anyone, even adults, can remake their executive function skills.

In our city case study on Manila, we discussed how education provides one pathway off the cycle of poverty. Brain science takes that a step further. The rebuilding of EF skills requires more than tuition for school. Individuals who have underdeveloped EF skills also need one-on-one coaching and mentoring over long periods of time, as well as an understanding support network that knows the best strategies to develop executive function skills. *Crittenton Women's Union*'s "Using Brain Science to Design New Pathways Out of Poverty" advocates for "interventions that allow individual participants to exercise choice" and "educating staff about the special EF challenges low-income families [and individuals] face … [which] can improve staff interactions with clients and the quality of program delivery."

Change starts with understanding. We need to keep building paths off the cycle of poverty, and one way we do that is by understanding the brain science behind poverty. Once we develop that understanding, we can move toward creating and developing more programs that address those specific needs.

BRICK BY BRICK: BUILDING SAFE SPACES

The slums of Manila are unsafe for maturing homeless teenagers who need a healthy home environment. The adult shelters of New York City are unsafe for LGBTQIA+ homeless youth who face discriminatory practices. The streets of Nairobi are unsafe for the homeless girls preyed upon by men. For too many homeless teenagers, safe shelter feels—and is—unattainable. This needs to change.

Safe, permanent shelter should be available to anyone in need, especially teenagers who are already dealing with the stress of growing up. Building safe spaces also begins with our understanding of the specific needs of those who lack a permanent, safe shelter. What teens need to feel safe shifts for different groups of homeless youth.

In a 2008 *Family Court Review* research article, "Making Homeless Youth Housing Safer for Lesbian, Gay, Bisexual, and Transgender Youth," Ernst Hunter examined some specific criteria that made housing safer for LGBTQIA+ teenagers. Several strategies were proposed.

First, shelters should provide private showers versus group showers. Hunter noted that group showering can "precipitate the assault" of LGBTQIA+ youth by people who react to differences between themselves and others in violent and inappropriate ways. This feels like a small change but would significantly increase the safety of LGBTQIA+ youth.

Second, staff at shelters should be provided with nondiscrimination and sensitivity training. Understanding is the foundation for change, and helping shelter staff understand the specific challenges faced by LGBTQIA+ homeless youth would hopefully enable staff members to provide respectful, compassionate care. Also, Hunter notes that studies show that LGBTQIA+ youth are "less likely than others to report violence against themselves," noting that "by creating an environment in which [LGBTQIA+] youth feel they are respected by the staff, [it will be] more likely that [LGBTQIA+ youth] will report violence against themselves."

Third, Hunter advocates for the creation of programs dedicated to caring for and addressing the needs of LGBTQIA+ youth. Programs for LGBTQIA+ youth are effective at curbing violence against this vulnerable group of the homeless population, especially as they build a community of LGBTQIA+ youth who are facing similar struggles. This can help create a supportive network for young teenagers.

These ideas are not necessarily huge innovations, but crucially, all changes consider the experiences and feelings of LGBTQIA+ homeless youth. To continue the building of safe spaces for homeless teenagers, we need to listen to their needs—and then develop spaces and programs that address those needs in a meaningful and respectful manner.

Avenues for Homeless Youth runs this Minneapolis shelter. Their mission is to provide "a safe and nurturing environment" so youth can "achieve their personal goals."

STORY BY STORY: INFORMING PUBLIC PERCEPTION

Homelessness is commonly misunderstood. Public opinion usually veers toward believing homeless youth are delinquents, rather than understanding the nuances behind their individual stories. One of the best ways to move forward and combat homelessness is to tell and hear the stories of homeless youth around the world. Actively listening and understanding the specific challenges they face helps inform public perception.

This means real, actionable change in policies can come from a place of understanding.

As social media increases its presence in our lives, one man has found a way to use Facebook to share the stories of homeless individuals and families in Naiorbi on a global scale.

Sham Patel was born and raised in Kenya's capital but had never paid much attention to the homeless population of his city. Then, a chance encounter changed his perspective. Now, he seeks to provide a "virtual home" for the stories of people living on the streets of the Kenyan capital:

> Ever since I was young, I've seen homeless people on the streets of Nairobi. They have become part of the wallpaper of this city. For a long time, I didn't see them as people but as pests who bother people for money. We're conditioned to think like that by an apathetic society from when we're young. We're pre-programmed.

Then, on his way to the gym, Sham glimpsed a huddle of homeless adults who were trying to stay dry from the rain under a plastic sheet. He said:

> It made me think about how I'd feel if that was me or my parents out in the rain without shelter and food. I decided then that it was time to try to make a small difference where possible so the next day I took them bread and milk and started a conversation with them … They shared the bread with me. In fact, they offered it to me first before they ate. Since then, I've decided to talk to and spread the stories of as many

homeless people as possible with the hope that we can build a movement that will lead to finding ways to help these men, women and children that much of society and our government has discarded.

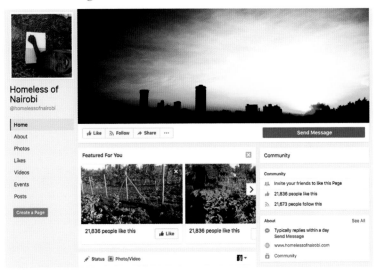

The Homeless of Nairobi Facebook page aims to promote understanding and compassion through the stories it shares.

Sham's Facebook page is still up and running, named Homeless of Nairobi, and it shares photos, conversations, and project updates, all meant to give insight into the lives of homeless youth and adults in Nairobi. His project encourages donations and a deeper understanding of the difficulties faced by the homeless Kenyan population.

At a glance, sharing stories is a simple idea. But our stories help us glimpse and understand the connections between us and those less fortunate. And it's these connections that enhance our empathy and compassion, hopefully altering any preconceived prejudices we might have.

RECOGNIZING AND BUILDING POTENTIAL

A second, crucial component of listening to and understanding the stories of homeless youth around the world is to recognize each teenager's individual potential. Listening to their stories, hopes, and aspirations gives us insight into how to help homeless teenagers recognize and build up their own potential. And by investing resources in the potential of our youth, we are investing resources in a future of opportunities for them.

Several studies have pointed out the importance of grit and resilience in teenagers. This is especially true for teenagers who find themselves without safe, permanent shelter. In a 2008 *American Journal of Orthopsychiatry* article, "Resilience in Homeless Youth: The Key Role of Self-Esteem," Dr. Sean Kidd discussed the importance and life-saving nature of resilience in teenagers. Kidd pointed out several studies that acknowledge that, for homeless youth, the "greater frequency and intensity of abuse and neglect by caregivers have been shown to be related to poor mental health and victimization on the street." He also states that the "experience of feeling/being trapped, similar to the experience of helplessness, has been identified ... as being the core element of emotional distress experienced by homeless youth and a key precipitant of suicide attempts."

Kidd is describing one of the core emotional struggles of homeless teenagers: feeling trapped and helpless in their situation. These are overwhelming emotions. When a teenager feels like there's no way to change their living situation, this mentality keeps them from seeking new opportunities or believing in their own abilities. However, a teenager who has developed their resilience and knows how to bounce back from a challenge or tragedy is more equipped mentally and emotionally to move their life forward.

Many organizations are dedicated to building the self-esteem and resilience of homeless teenagers. Often, their programs are built upon creative expression, a wonderful way to give homeless youth an outlet for to tell their own stories. One organization that is making strides to help homeless teenagers find their own voice is New York City's Art Start. Launched in 1991, the organization uses the creative arts to "transform young, at-risk lives." They provide daily creative arts workshops, where local artists and educators donate their time to foster the creative expression of at-risk youth. Art Start's goal is to "instill in … youth the confidence to appreciate who they already are and what they innately have to offer the world; then, to think critically, ask important questions, and pursue meaningful opportunities in life."

For many of the youth enrolled in Art Start's workshops, this chance to be creative within a supportive mainframe provides them a sense of consistency and direction, both of which build resilience in these teenagers. Another crucial element of Art Start is that they go to at-risk youth, hosting the workshops where at-risk youth are to encourage participation. This way at-risk youth who may have closed themselves off from help have the chance to engage in the workshops.

A huge part of why Art Start succeeds is because it builds connections between homeless youth and their community. We all have a role in how our communities help and address homelessness. A simple, but major, step forward is encouraging respectful and caring connections that help homeless youth recognize their potential within.

"SOLVING" HOMELESSNESS—FOR GOOD

Is there truly a solution to "solve" homelessness? Various groups in America say it's possible—but it requires an investment of resources, as well as a multi-pronged strategy.

Solutions for Change, a San Diego organization, is a nonprofit with a business-like approach to "transforming lives in 1,000 days." To help families permanently get off the streets, they offer more than a simple housing solution. They provide affordable housing, but Solutions for Change also mandates that all adult participants must attend their Solutions University, a "full service leadership development residential program." This program "equips parents with the skills, knowledge, and resources to completely transform themselves and their families." The organization's services include counseling sessions, job training, and parenting classes. A vast and varied support network made of staff members and volunteers offers considerable support and encouragement to the families who are piecing their lives back together.

The nonprofit recognizes that each family will have their own journey, and each has specific needs. However, ensuring their participants are emotionally and mentally prepared to rebuild their lives ensures success. Since 1999, Solutions for Change has helped almost eight hundred families go "from homelessness to self-sufficiency."

The "solution" to homelessness means looking at the issue from every angle. Simply addressing a person's need for shelter is almost never the full answer to helping someone get off the streets. Homelessness is a complicated issue that requires innovative strategies to solve—and, for Solutions for Change, their system is one that is working very well for families looking to break out of the cycle of homelessness.

San Diego has a large homeless population. Solutions for Change is one nonprofit based there that aims to solve the problem through a holistic approach.

THE MOVERS AND SHAKERS

While the above ideas are large-scale changes, big differences can also launch with a single person with a singular idea. History has relied on movers and shakers to re-write its stories. Here are a couple of the forward thinkers who are finding ways to lend a hand around the world.

KESZ VALDEZ

Cris "Kesz" Valdez knows exactly what it's like living on the streets in the Philippines. Throughout his childhood, Kesz himself was homeless, living off the bits and pieces he found scavenging through garbage heaps and sleeping in cemetery tombs. When he was seven years old, Kesz founded his charity, Championing Community Children (C3), with the simple goal of enabling homeless Filipino children to practice basic hygiene. As discussed in our Manila case study, one of the greatest hazards to youth living on the streets of the Philippines is the daily risks to their health. This comes from the toxic living conditions of the slums, but it also applies to a lack of access to personal hygiene products among homeless Filipino youth.

Kesz sought to remedy this. Homeless at the age of two, he was kicked out of his family home. Badly burned in a dumpster fire, a social worker gave him a home and the opportunity to leave the streets. But Kesz never forgot the personal experiences of his fellow peers on the streets. When he turned seven, his birthday wish was not for himself—instead, he asked for gifts to give homeless youth in his city. Nicknamed "Hope Gifts," Kesz's gift packages contain basic hygiene products (like toothbrushes and soap), flip-flops (to protect the feet of children scavenging for food), clothing, and toys.

Kesz's assistance began to expand further. Along with the gifts, he started teaching homeless youth how to take care of themselves. "I teach the children how to wash hands properly, brush their teeth daily, and bathe regularly," he said.

Since he began Championing Community Children, Kesz has helped more than ten thousand children. In 2012, he was awarded the International Children's Peace Prize for his

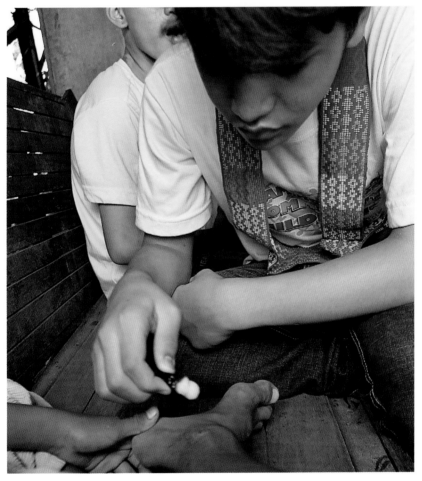

Kesz Valdez helps clean the wound of a homeless boy in the Philippines.

dedication to helping the homeless youth of the Philippines. In his speech, he declared, "Our health is our wealth! Being healthy will enable you to play, to think clearly, to get up and go to school and love the people around you in so many ways."

Kesz is a caring beacon of hope for many homeless teenagers in his community. Not only is he providing products to help Filipino youth dodge health hazards, he also builds connections with them, letting them know they're not alone in the world.

NADYA OKAMOTO

Menstruation is typically a topic we shy away from in public discourse. Nadya Okamoto is seeking to change this aversion with her company, PERIOD.

As a sixteen-year-old teenager, Nadya was in and out of shelters as her family struggled with money issues. One weekend, Nadya was on her own at a women's shelter. During her conversations with the women at the shelter, she discovered many struggled with how to deal with their monthly menstruation. They barely had enough money for food. Menstruation products—which could cost them half their food budget—were simply out of the question. Instead, the women used pieces of cloth and cleaned themselves with sponges.

For Nadya, it had never occurred to her that some individuals who menstruate wouldn't be able to afford menstruation products. And, without those products, dealing with a monthly period in a sanitary and effective way became a lot more challenging. Nadya decided this needed to change.

Nadya launched her company, then named Camions of Care, which began providing period packs to people who couldn't afford them. The nonprofit organization, now named PERIOD, seeks to serve, educate, and advocate. They still hand out period packs but are also working toward changing the conversation on periods, seeking to "eliminate the taboo [of talking about periods] through a growing network of high school, college,

Nadya Okamoto (*center*) is focused on a future where "those in need" have the menstruation products they require.

and community chapters." They also "raise awareness and create change through events, campaigns, and media relationships."

Nadya firmly believes that menstrual care is a basic right. PERIOD is a fierce advocate for those who menstruate, fighting for their right to have the materials to menstruate with dignity and without hazard to their health.

HOW CAN *WE* HELP?

Teenagers without permanent, safe shelter are not victims or individuals who need "saving." Studies have shown that the best way to help homeless youth is to treat them with dignity and respect, include them within their greater community, and build their resilience and grit. This respect and valuing of them as individuals will help empower many to build a self-sufficient lifestyle. But, of course, this is only part of the solution. Often, outside help is also needed. Change must come from higher up, with effective policy changes that specifically address the needs of homeless teenagers.

However, one powerful way for us to effect change is to quite simply start the conversation. Hear the stories of homeless teenagers in your community. Learn about ways you can help. Then, share that knowledge with your friends and family. It's time for us to focus the conversation on teenage homelessness. Then and only then will we be able find solutions, alter rooted bias, and build toward a future where every teenager has a place to call home.

GLOSSARY

adapt To alter the way you behave so that it is easier to live in a certain place or situation.

advocates People who passionately back and defend a cause.

affluent Having a significant amount of wealth.

child welfare system A set of government services that are intended to keep children safe and give families the support needed to care for their children.

cost-burdened Percentage of household income spent on a mortgage or monthly rent. According to HUD programs, households spending more than 30 percent of income for these housing costs are considered to be "cost-burdened." Households spending more than 50 percent are considered to be "severely cost-burdened."

couch surfers Those who stay overnight in someone else's home, typically on their host's couch.

crisis beds Temporary, short-term housing to help an individual who needs immediate shelter, usually in an emergency.

disempowered A descriptor for when an individual or group is less likely than others to succeed and have power.

executive function (EF) skills A set of skills made up of three main skills: impulse control, working memory, and mental flexibility.

gender identity An individual's internal sense of being male, female, neither, or somewhere in between.

globalization The process of involving the entire global community.

gross domestic product The value of a country's produced goods and provided services in a single year.

infrastructure The structures a city, country, or area needs to operate, such as bridges and roads.

LGBTQIA+ An acronym that stands for Lesbian, Gay, Bisexual, Transgender, Queer or Questioning, Intersex, Asexual, and + for all other sexualities, sexes, and genders that aren't represented in these letters.

perceptions The way an individual understands someone or something.

pervasive Something that has spread to all areas of an item or concept.

Point-in-Time Counts A count of the sheltered and unsheltered homeless population in America on a January night.

poverty The state of being poor and not having enough money for basic necessities.

poverty line The level of income that makes it possible for a person to pay for basic food, clothing, and shelter in their country.

resilience The ability to regain your strength, health, or success following difficult circumstances.

sexual orientation An individual's sexual preference or identity as bisexual, heterosexual, asexual, homosexual, or somewhere along the spectrum.

stability The state of being difficult to change.

stigma Negative opinions that some individuals have about something or a group of people.

street children Unsupervised youth who spend most of their time on the streets. The streets are either their home and/or where they earn income.

survival sex Trading sex acts to meet their needs for food, shelter, etc.

susceptible Easy to affect or influence.

tenacity Possessing incredible determination to accomplish something.

transient Not permanent, not staying in one place for long.

work ethic A dedication to working hard, coupled with a belief in the value of work to build character.

working poor Individuals who are part of the working community but earn very little money and are unable to pay for expensive goods or services.

Books

Berg, Ryan. *No House to Call My Home: Love, Family, and Other Transgressions*. New York: Nation Books, 2015.

Murray, Liz. *Breaking Night: A Memoir of Forgiveness, Survival, and My Journey from Homeless to Harvard*. New York: Hachette Books, 2010.

Ryan, Kevin, and Tina Kelley. *Almost Home: Helping Kids Move from Homelessness to Hope*. Hoboken, NJ: Wiley, 2012.

Websites

Art Start
http://www.art-start.org/

Art Start is an organization that holds art workshops in homeless shelters. Explore their website to learn more about the art projects they've spearheaded and to see examples of artwork that promotes the visibility of homeless teens.

Covenant House: New York
https://ny.covenanthouse.org

Learn more about homeless teens living in New York City and find out about ways that you can help.

Kenya Children of Hope

http://kenyachildrenofhope.org/

Read more stories about the homeless teens of Nairobi and learn about how the charitable organization Kenya Children of Hope helps teens and children find stable housing and opportunity.

Videos

"Lifestory Kesz Valdez, The International Children's Peace Prize Winner 2012"

https://www.youtube.com/watch?v=nQDv62yQ_t0

This short video profiles Kesz Valdez, the 2012 International Children's Peace Prize winner, who fights for the rights of street children in the Philippines.

"The Woman Who Gives FREE Sanitary Products to the Homeless"

https://www.youtube.com/watch?v=j88sOT1SBqk

Learn more about Nadaya Okamoto, a young woman who, at sixteen years old, launched an organization that provides menstrual products to homeless individuals who need them.

BIBLIOGRAPHY

Alegado, Siegfrid, and Cecilia Yap. "Philippines Posts Strongest Economic Growth in Asia at 7.1%." *Bloomberg*, November 17, 2016. https://www.bloomberg.com/news/articles/2016-11-17/philippine-growth-quickens-to-7-1-on-duterte-s-spending-spree.

Babcock, Elisabeth D. "Using Brain Science to Design New Pathways Out of Poverty." *Crittenton Women's Union*, 2014. http://s3.amazonaws.com/empath-website/pdf/Research-UsingBrainScienceDesignPathwaysPoverty-0114.pdf.

Brown, Andy. "Real Lives - A Day in the Life: Crisanto's Story." *UNICEF Philippines*. Retrieved April 4, 2017. https://www.unicef.org/philippines/reallives_14587.html.

———. "Real Lives - A Day in the Life: Mary's Story. " *UNICEF Philippines*. Retrieved April 4, 2017. https://www.unicef.org/philippines/reallives_14588.html.

Coalition for the Homeless. "Basic Facts About Homelessness: New York City." Retrieved April 4, 2017. http://www.coalitionforthehomeless.org/basic-facts-about-homelessness-new-york-city/.

————. "The Callahan Legacy: *Callahan v. Carey* and the Legal Right to Shelter." Retrieved April 10, 2017. http://www.coalitionforthehomeless.org/our-programs/advocacy/legal-victories/the-callahan-legacy-callahan-v-carey-and-the-legal-right-to-shelter/.

Covenant House. "Alone in the Cold." September 12, 2012. https://www.covenanthouse.org/homeless-kids/alone-cold.

————. "Statistics on Homeless Youth in America." Last modified October 20, 2016. https://www.covenanthouse.org/homeless-teen-issues/statistics.

Daily Nation. "Tough life for street children in Kenya." April 14, 2016. http://www.nation.co.ke/news/Street-children-struggle-for-survival-in-Kenya/1056-3158442-147dkpdz/index.html.

Fihlani, Pumza. "Feeding Kenya's Street Kids: An Evening with Nairobi's 'Messiah.'" *BBC News*, May 2, 2015. http://www.bbc.com/news/world-africa-31359061.

Forbes. "This Organization Could Have the Answer to Solve Homelessness." January 19, 2017. https://www.forbes.com/sites/opportunitylives/2017/01/19/this-organization-could-have-the-answer-to-solve-homelessness/#2a6d13dd4040.

Gay, Mara. "Most New Yorkers Believe Homelessness Has Become Worse under de Blasio." *Wall Street Journal,* January 19, 2017. https://www.wsj.com/articles/most-new-yorkers-believe-homelessness-has-become-worse-under-de-blasio-1484855052.

HUD. "Affordable Housing." Retrieved April 3, 2017. https://portal.hud.gov/hudportal/HUD?src=/program_offices/comm_planning/affordablehousing/.

IRIN. "IRIN – Youth in Crisis – Coming of Age in the 21st Century." February 2007. http://www.newunionism.net/library/internationalism/IRIN%20-%20Youth%20in%20Crisis%20-%20Coming%20of%20Age%20in%20the%2021st%20Century%20-%202007.pdf.

Make Them Visible. "Make Them Visible." Retrieved April 6, 2017. http://makethemvisible.com/.

McKenzie, David. "Kenya's Street Teens Struggle to Survive." CNN, November 6, 2009. http://us.cnn.com/2009/WORLD/africa/11/06/kenya.street.survivors/index.html.

Medina, Sarah. "Kesz Valdez: Homeless Filipino Boy Wins $130,000 Children's Peace Prize." *Huffington Post*, September 25, 2012. http://www.huffingtonpost.com/2012/09/25/kesz-valdez-_n_1910737.html.

National Network for Youth. "Consequences of Youth Homelessness." Retrieved April 8, 2017. https://www.nn4youth.org/wp-content/uploads/IssueBrief_Youth_Homelessness.pdf.

———. "Why Do Young People Become Homeless in America?" Retrieved April 4, 2017. https://www.nn4youth.org/learn/why-homeless/.

PERIOD. "Leading the Menstrual Movement." Retrieved April 10, 2017. https://www.period.org/about-us/.

Selinger, Rolando. "Nairobi's Social Outcasts Children Addicted to Glue." *The Grass Roots Journal*, September 2, 2015. http://www.thegrassrootsjournal.org/single-post/2015/9/1/Nairobis-Social-Outcasts-Children-Addicted-to-Glue.

Siciliano, Carl. "Three LGBT Youths Describe Being Homeless in NYC." *ADVOCATE*, December 21, 2015. http://www.advocate.com/commentary/2015/12/21/three-lgbt-youths-describe-being-homeless-nyc.

Smith, David. "Homeless of Nairobi: Facebook Project Gives Rough Sleepers a Voice." *The Guardian*, January 19, 2015. https://www.theguardian.com/world/2015/jan/19/-sp-homeless-nairobi-facebook-project-gives-rough-sleepers-voice.

Solutions for Change. "Solutions for Change." Retrieved April 10, 2017. http://solutionsforchange.org/.

Tantiangco, Aya. "Rodallie Mosende Changes the Way We See Homelessness." *GMA News Online*, May 23, 2016. http://www.gmanetwork.com/news/story/567289/ lifestyle/artandculture/rodallie-mosende-changes-the-way-we-see-homelessness.

United Nations Educational, Scientific and Cultural Organization. "Street Children." Retrieved April 3, 2017. http://www.unesco.org/new/en/social-and-human-sciences/themes/fight-against-discrimination/education-of-children-in-need/street-children/.

Villamor, Felipe, and Russell Goldman. "Fire Tears Through Manila Slum, Leaving 15,000 Homeless." *New York Times*, February 8, 2017. https://www.nytimes.com/2017/02/08/ world/asia/fire-tears-through-manila-slum-leaving-15000-homeless.html.

Weller, Chris. "Manila Is the Most Crowded City in the World—Here's What Life Is Like." *Business Insider*, August 4, 2016. http://www.businessinsider.com/manila-worlds-most-crowded-city-2016-8.

Westhead, Rick. "What Sustains Homeless Teens in Manila: Karaoke." *TheStar.com*. Last modified May 17, 2014. https://www.thestar.com/news/world/2014/05/17/what_sustains_homeless_teens_in_manila_karaoke.html.

Youth.gov. "Homelessness and Runaway." Retrieved April 3, 2017. http://youth.gov/youth-topics/runaway-and-homeless-youth.

INDEX

Page numbers in **boldface** are illustrations. Entries in **boldface** are glossary terms.

ABOUT THE AUTHOR

Monika Davies is a Canadian writer and traveler. She's been writing since she could define "exposition" and graduated from the University of British Columbia with a BFA in creative writing. She has written more than eighteen books for young readers, including *No Way! Spectacular Sports Stories*, *True Life: Alexander Hamilton*, *Surprising Things We Eat*, *California Gold Rush*, and *The Hidden World of Toilets*.